BRIAN JOHNSTON

Minutes to Midnight

The Bible's Prophetic Clock

HAYES PRESS

First published by Hayes Press 2023

Copyright © 2023 by Brian Johnston

All rights reserved. No part of this publication may be reproduced, stored or transmitted in any form or by any means, electronic, mechanical, photocopying, recording, scanning, or otherwise without written permission from the publisher. It is illegal to copy this book, post it to a website, or distribute it by any other means without permission.

Unless otherwise stated, all Bible quotations are taken from the (NASB®) New American Standard Bible®, Copyright © 1960, 1971, 1977, 1995, 2020 by The Lockman Foundation. Used by permission. All rights reserved. lockman.org

Quotations marked NKJV are taken from the New King James Version®. Copyright © 1982 by Thomas Nelson. Used by permission. All rights reserved.

Quotations marked NIV are taken from the Holy Bible, New International Version®, NIV®. Copyright © 1973, 1978, 1984, 2011 by Biblica, Inc.™ Used by permission of Zondervan. All rights reserved worldwide. www.zondervan.com The "NIV" and "New International Version" are trademarks registered in the United States Patent and Trademark Office by Biblica, Inc.™

First edition

This book was professionally typeset on Reedsy.
Find out more at reedsy.com

Contents

1

Are We Nearly There?

Towards the end of 2023, world news was dominated by events in the Gaza Strip that were triggered when Hamas gunmen launched an unprecedented assault on Israel from the Gaza Strip on 7 October, killing more than 1,400 people and taking 230 hostages. Hamas, as is well known, is a Palestinian group that has ruled the Gaza Strip since 2007. The group is sworn to Israel's destruction and wants to replace it with an Islamic state. Hamas has fought several wars with Israel since it took power. It has fired – or allowed other groups to fire – thousands of rockets into Israel, and has carried out other deadly attacks. In response, Israel has repeatedly attacked Hamas with air strikes. In 2008 and 2014, Israel also sent troops into Gaza.

For students of Bible prophecy there are two points to note from these recent tragic events. First, the precise location of the Gaza Strip was prophesied by various Bible prophets more than two and a half thousand years ago that it would undergo violence in the time of the end. This, as we are all too painfully aware, is now happening before our eyes when we view daily television news reports. We do well to seriously consider the implications of this.

The second point of note is that the countries surrounding Israel and currently hostile to her, were singled out in the Bible by numerous prophets as being the targets of divine judgement for the hatred they show towards Israel. The Bible mentions them by their ancient names. They've hated Israel before and have already been judged historically for that same hatred. But the Bible passages involving these ancient enemies also contain clear indications that similar hostility would continue and their final judgement is reserved for what is known as the Day of the Lord. That's a term that occurs around 25 times in the Old Testament, and refers to the time when the Lord Jesus will return to earth to judge the nations and establish his just rule.

In making this claim about how we can connect the nations named in the Bible with their modern counterparts, we're using the method of interpretation that first identifies the exact geographical areas the Bible refers to in history by their ancient names, and then we simply update those same regions by calling them by their modern names. First of all then, let's return to the point about the Gaza Strip being the subject of Bible prophecy relating to what's known as the end times. From the prophet Ezekiel in chapter 25, we read:

> *"This is what the Lord GOD says: 'Because the Philistines have acted in revenge, and have taken vengeance with malice in their souls to destroy with everlasting hostility," therefore this is what the Lord GOD says: "Behold, I am*

going to reach out with My hand against the Philistines and eliminate the Cherethites; and I will destroy the remnant of the seacoast. I will execute great vengeance on them with wrathful rebukes; and they will know that I am the LORD, when I inflict My vengeance on them.'"

Those are verses 15 to 17. What's striking about this is the way it's worded in terms of the personal intervention of the Lord. He'll personally inflict his vengeance on the Philistines, the Cherethites and the remnant of the seacoast. In historical biblical geography, these terms are very definitely associated with the south-western coastland of Israel. And this is the region familiar to us today as the Palestinian territories and notably the Gaza Strip. Turning now to the Bible prophet Zephaniah and chapter two, after an ominous mention of 'the day of the Lord's anger' in verse two, the recipients of this are identified from verses 4-7:

"For Gaza will be abandoned, And Ashkelon will become a desolation; The inhabitants of Ashdod will be driven out at noon, And Ekron will be uprooted. Woe to the inhabitants of the seacoast, The nation of the Cherethites! The word of the LORD is against you, Canaan, land of the Philistines; And I will eliminate you So that there will be no inhabitant. So the seacoast will become grazing places, With pastures for shepherds and folds for flocks. And the coast will be For the remnant of the house of Judah, They will drive sheep to pasture on it. In the houses of Ashkelon they will lie down at evening; For the LORD their God will care for them And restore their fortunes."

In this example, it's arresting to observe the place name of Gaza being explicitly mentioned as typical of the cities of the ancient Cherethite nation of the land of the Philistines in the Mediterranean seacoast of southern Israel. Most readers of the Bible will relate to Israel's young anointed king, David, in his epic dispatch of the Philistine giant, Goliath. The rather more flawed hero, Samson, was once trapped in Gaza for a short while. Joshua's conquering forces had failed to completely overrun the area of the Philistines and the cities named here, with the result that they became a thorn in Israel's flesh. David, at times, allied himself with them when Saul was jealously pursuing him after identifying him as the main rival to his throne. And it was from there that David would draw a unit of brave fighters to serve as his bodyguards under Benaiah (1 Samuel 30:14; 2 Samuel 8:18; 15:18; 20:17, 23).

If the back of your Bible contains some Bible maps, you can easily identify where these names are located and check they identify with the area of the modern Gaza Strip. Finally, let's turn to Joel's prophecy, chapter 3, and the first 4 verses:

> *"For behold, in those days and at that time, when I restore the fortunes of Judah and Jerusalem, I will gather all the nations and bring them down to the Valley of Jehoshaphat. Then I will enter into judgment with them there on behalf of My people and My inheritance, Israel, whom they have scattered among the nations; and they have divided up My land. They have also cast lots for My people, traded a boy for a prostitute, and sold a girl for wine so that they may drink. Moreover, what are you to Me, Tyre, Sidon,*

and all the regions of Philistia? Are you repaying Me with retribution? But if you are showing Me retribution, swiftly and speedily I will return your retribution on your head!"

Notice how it's said that Israel will be divided up or partitioned. This statement has modern origins. Between the 1920s and 1940s, the number of Jews arriving back in their old homeland grew, with many fleeing from persecution in Europe, and especially from the Nazi Holocaust in World War Two. Violence between Jews and Arabs, and against British rule, also increased. In 1947, the United Nations voted for Palestine to be split into separate Jewish and Arab states. This proved problematic to say the least. The British withdrew, Israel declared its independence, and the very next day was attacked by five Arab countries determined to annihilate it. Hundreds of thousands of Palestinians fled or were told by the aggressors to leave their homes so as not to get caught up in what was to be Israel's intended destruction. But by the time the fighting ended in a ceasefire the following year, Israel controlled most of the territory. And so arose the Palestinian refugee problem we hear so much of today. It's this problem that's at the heart of recent and ongoing events.

And it's here in Joel that we also find an interesting extension of the prophesied final judgement on the areas we've already been tracking. That's because Tyre and Sidon also feature. These place names equate with modern-day Lebanon. It's from there that the group Hezbollah are joining the attack on Israel. In other words, we identify the operational bases of Hamas and Hezbollah in the writing of the prophet Joel. The trading of

Israeli children does uncomfortably evoke the images we've been seeing of child hostages among the more than 200 taken on October 7. After prophesying the coming judgment against the Antichrist, Isaiah, in chapters 13 through 23, gives us a list of many nations to be destroyed or judged along with the Antichrist when the Messiah comes to bring the victory that's long been promised to his people. And included among them, Isaiah also contains mention of judgement against the southwestern seacoast of Israel in his chapter 14:

> "Wail, you gate; cry, you city; Melt away, Philistia, all of you! For smoke comes from the north, And there is no straggler in his ranks. What answer will one give the messengers of the nation? That the LORD has founded Zion, And the poor of His people will take refuge in it" (vv.31,32).

It's hard to disassociate the imagery of smoke from the north and no straggler in his ranks from the aerial bombardment and massive ground force invasion we've witnessed. Of course, whether something even more climactic awaits this wretched region remains to be seen. The fact that Isaiah includes this particular detail alongside his reference to the Antichrist (whose motif in his writing is 'the Assyrian'), most clearly points us to the future. That's why we may ask the question: 'Are we nearly there?' The modern counterpart nations awaiting God's judgment in the Bible time of the end, as mentioned not only by Isaiah but also by a good number of Old Testament prophets, all share a common religious hatred of Israel.

2

The Mother of All Prophecy

It's been called the mother of all prophecy and the first preaching of the Gospel. What is it? Well, you've probably guessed that I'm referring to Genesis 3 verse 15 (NIV): *"And I will put enmity between you and the woman, and between your offspring and hers; He will crush [strike, Mgn.] your head, and you will strike his heel."* Perhaps, we should begin by reviewing what led to God saying this. Context, after all, is king when it comes to figuring out what any Bible verse means. We find ourselves back in the Garden of Eden. The first man whom God created, and his helper, Eve, are standing before God. But, another creature is present. He's only described in the book of Genesis as a snake or serpent. Not until we reach the New Testament, do we find him identified as Satan, otherwise known as the Devil. Some time before, in Genesis chapter 1, God had pronounced his creation of the heavens and the earth to be very good. God had simply spoken and it was done. No processes known to us that we can determine were involved. But, by that moment in time, back in Genesis chapter 3, the original perfection of God's creation has been shattered. As has recurred so often since, a human blunder was even then responsible for the unending misery that would unfold.

In a straightforward test of obedience, our first parents failed disastrously in a catastrophe of cosmic proportions. Since this is written in the Bible in classic historic narrative style, we accept the plain sense of the Text. There was a first man created by God from the dust of the earth, for we're certainly comprised of the same chemical elements that are to be found in the earth. Adam was the very first man, unique at this time, and created in the image of his creator, God. As a result of human rebellion against God's command not to eat the fruit of just one exceptional tree in the Garden, mortality was decreed upon Adam and all his posterity. His spiritual relationship with God also died that day. He'd been taken from the ground and to the ground he'd now return in due course. This is something we acknowledge in funeral services to this day: that dust returns to dust. The sober and literal truth of the fulfilment of this part of our decreed fate leaves no room for any merely poetic understanding of how it was that we were formed from dust in the first place.

The first ever Garden now becomes a courtroom, and God announced his verdict on the now guilty pairing of the very first man and wife to grace, or rather disgrace, the planet. Let's hear that verdict again: *"And I will put enmity between you and the woman, and between your offspring and hers; He will crush [strike, Mgn.] your head, and you will strike his heel"* (NIV). My attention has been drawn to the observation that this mother of all prophecy, this first sounding of God's Good News of hope for humanity, is in three parts. Looking at it now, this does seem to be the case. And so here, in the midst of the story of Adam and

Eve, standing together with Satan the serpent, in this one single verse, God gave an overview of the whole of redemptive history.

In the first part, the sentence is addressed to Satan but concerns Eve, the mother of all humanity. She became a sinner, and God declared from that day forward there would be hostility between herself and Satan. And indeed, what heartache she would soon come to know when her firstborn turned upon and murdered his younger brother! But there's more to this first prophecy. We now come to part two. Beyond this, Satan's offspring or followers would be at enmity with the offspring of Eve who don't follow Satan. Perhaps, we can think of her offspring as first being her godly seed through Seth, later becoming the true natural descendants of Abraham, together in time with those who'd become his spiritual descendants through their faith in Christ.

Possibly, among other things that come to mind as we reflect on this, are the Lord's words denouncing disbelieving Jews as being "*of their father the Devil*" (John 8:44). They weren't true Jews: they weren't Jews inwardly. Beyond that, what also may come to mind could be the text from Revelation chapter 12 about how in a future time, Satan will make war with the woman and "*the children of the woman*" – where the woman in question is neither Eve nor Mary but the nation of true-hearted Israelites (v.17). Those who hold the testimony of Jesus are included as 'the rest of her children.' Satan will at that time be working through his own followers, led by the Antichrist. The attack is against all who profess Jesus as God's Messiah. And so, overall, an ages-long struggle is predicted that may help explain both anti-Semitic hostility and the persecution of Christians in its various forms. Satan's offspring or followers could be thought of as celestial as well as those here on earth, with at times a strong interaction, for Paul says our wrestling is against spiritual hosts of wickedness (Ephesians 6). Such dark forces were also revealed by the prophet Daniel as forces arrayed against Daniel's people, the Jews, when at that time also hostilities were being played out on earth.

The attacks by Hamas terrorists on the 7th October, 2023, have been styled by some as being 'Israel's 9/11'. Israel's defence forces retaliated with overwhelming force, to the dismay of many in the international community. Mass protests took place in major western cities, notably London and Paris. At times, as many as 300,000 pro-Palestinian protesters were marching in the streets of UK cities. There was an upsurge in anti-Semitic feeling, including in the United States. All that's contained in the first and second parts of the prophecy that is Genesis 3:15. But there's a third part, and this is where the hope of salvation is announced. It's in the third part of the prophecy, that I suggest the war is made much more specific. For we're told, in particular, that Satan would be in combat with the "Seed," which is the Messiah.

Generally, we may say that according to this ancient prophecy, the developing history of this planet would prove to be the story of the people of Satan in conflict with the people of God. But then, in the third part, comes the glorious promise that although Satan would merely bruise – or strike – the heel of the Messiah, at the cross; the Messiah will crush the head of Satan there. From the very beginning of humanity's long history, God declared that Eve's singular 'seed,' the Messiah, would make right the damage done on that very sad and dark day in the Garden. In fact, more than make it right! It's so concise, but in a single verse, in one brief declaration, we have a synopsis of all of redemptive history. It's this prophecy that gives birth to all the other prophetic promises in the Bible regarding the Messiah. Biblical prophecy relates also to Israel, and I invite you to check for yourself if the nations surrounding Israel today, mostly sharing a border with her, nations united by a common religion, are not precisely those mentioned in ancient biblical prophecies such as Psalm 83.

3

The Final World Empire

Ever since I was a boy, I've loved the Bible book of Daniel, and stories such as his escape from a lions' den. I later became aware that there were people who treated the book of Daniel with suspicion. Was it genuine history or merely exaggerated stories? I remember being thrilled when hearing how archaeological discoveries had uncovered an artifact known as the Nabonidus cylinder. This object gave telling, even compelling, evidence to show that we can indeed put our trust in the book of Daniel – in its every word. The names on that cylinder's inscription established the co-regency of two kings (a father and son) at the time that fully justified Daniel being rewarded with the honour of becoming the third ruler in the Kingdom, as the Bible text had stated in Daniel 5:16. It's that attention to detail that confirms accuracy, allowing it to be fact-checked. One book once written as a reasoned defence of the book of Daniel was entitled 'Daniel in the Critics' Den.' I liked that. Daniel – or at least his book – had once again escaped unscathed!

The book of Daniel is a book of two halves. The first half is basically historical narrative. This is the part we use in Sunday Schools with children. The second half contains prophecy that takes us all the way to the time of the end, that is to the time of the end of this world's empires. They are brought to an end when Christ establishes his kingdom in this world. The book is also a book of two languages. It was written in Hebrew as was the vast majority of the Old Testament, but also partly in Aramaic, the international language at the time of writing. There is, naturally, a significance to this in that its prophetic outline spans two distinct programs. One program is for the Jewish people and the other program is for the international world at large. God was writing up history in advance. Before we say more about these programs, I'm interested to turn to Daniel's last chapter, chapter twelve. Here we are talking about the future time of the end of world empires:

> *"Now at that time Michael, the great prince who stands guard over the sons of your people, will arise. And there will be a time of distress such as never occurred since there was a nation until that time; and at that time your people, everyone who is found written in the book, will be rescued. And many of those who sleep in the dust of the ground will awake, these to everlasting life, but the others to disgrace and everlasting contempt. And those who have insight will shine like the glow of the expanse of heaven, and those who lead the many to righteousness, like the stars forever and ever. But as for you, Daniel, keep these words secret and seal up the book until the end of time; many will roam about, and knowledge will increase"* (Daniel 12:1-4).

This talks about a future time of distress for God's ancient people, Israel. It's worth making it clear that we don't believe in any so-called 'replacement theology' in which the Church, meaning all believers, has replaced Israel in God's plans. For now, Israel is set aside, as Paul argues in Romans (ch.11), but soon God will revive his dealings with his Old Testament people. He's certainly not broken – nor will he ever break – his literal promises to Abraham. His renewed dealings with Israel, however, will start with their purging or refining. A time of distress is predicted for Israel. What we see happening now is consistent with paving the way for that. In many places, anti-Semitic feeling is on the rise.

But then Daniel is told to keep these words secret, it's to be a closed book. Only at the time near to the end of world empires will the meaning of Daniel's writings become clear. I want to suggest that time is now. Daniel's prophecies have been variously interpreted. There have been some wild speculations. And there have also been carefully reasoned positions that have commanded respect, being worthy of consideration. But key information was not previously available. Immediately after saying that this writing of Daniel is to remain a closed book, we find the words: *"Many shall run to and fro, and knowledge shall increase."* This phrase has often, perhaps usually, been understood to be speaking of an increase of transportation and of the ease of access to information in the last days.

But is that what it means? It could make sense if understood that way, for sure. The world has shrunk in that we can jet around it and talk in terms of it becoming a global village. Computer power doubles every couple of years ('Moore's law') and now the concern is about taming the use of artificial intelligence or AI. But if we use the standard major key to unlock the interpretation of any verse – and that key is about observing its context – then we see that the words: *'Many shall run to and fro, and knowledge shall increase'*, follow on directly after the sealing up of Daniel's prophecy. This would indicate that the increasing knowledge can be seen instead as a reference to the gradual opening up of the prophecy by those who are diligently searching for understanding by scanning the pages of the Book of Daniel.

The running to and fro would then involve searching the book through and through, roaming backwards and forwards over its pages, scrutinizing it over and over until at last, at the end of the age, the book is finally unsealed and fully understood by the believing community. That explanation of this famous verse, I must say, commends itself to me. World concern is increasingly focused on the Middle East. The same geographical areas that were a threat to Israel in history are again a source of likely threat to that nation in modern times. In verse 9 of the same last chapter, Daniel is once again informed that the revelation given to him will not be fully understood until the time of the end. What's the point of this, we might ask ourselves? It means that the primary purpose of the revelation was to inform those who would live in the time of the end. Daniel himself was kept from understanding. Bible students 100 years or 80 years ago, perhaps even 20 years ago, couldn't know either.

Seventy-five years ago, Israel gained independence in its ancient homeland, or at least in part of it. And the last 20 years have seen the emergence of what's called the Islamic State. Emergence or should we say re-emergence? For the Islamic

Caliphate is the historical Islamic government or empire, which began (with the Rashidun Caliphate) in 632 AD, shortly after the death of Muhammad, the prophet of Islam. For a long time it endured and culminated in the Ottoman Empire, which officially came to an end in 1923, just one hundred years ago. The historical Islamic Caliphate fully, absolutely, completely conquered all the lands of the previous Babylonian, Medo-Persian and Greek empires (Daniel 2:40) and became a successor empire to them.

In contrast to the Roman Empire that tolerated the culture of those peoples it overran (as seen in the Gospels & Acts), and even built their roads, the Islamic Caliphate from its inception was a supremacist force that crushed and obliterated the cultures and religions of the peoples it conquered. This is due to the all-encompassing ideology of Islam, which includes every facet of life. It has rules and commandments that extend to far more than just theology; dictating the law, government, language, military, and even the sexual and hygienic practices of those under its authority. The very name Islam means 'submission.' Wherever Islam spread, it brought with it this oppressive ideology of submission. Islam conquered all the regions of the former Babylonian, Medo-Persian, and Grecian empires. It exported and imposed the Arabic language onto a vast proportion of its conquered peoples.

The messianic kingdom that Daniel saw coming in his visions specifically destroys the fourth world empire. But in doing so, we see that, by virtue of the destruction of this fourth empire or kingdom of the end-time Antichrist, then 'at the same time' Babylon, Medo-Persia, and Greece are also all destroyed (being the first three empires depicted as three metals of decreasing value): "*While you were watching, a rock was cut out, but not by human hands. It struck the statue on its feet of iron and clay and smashed them. Then the iron, the clay, the bronze, the silver and the gold were broken to pieces **at the same time** and became like chaff on a threshing floor in the summer. The wind swept them away without leaving a trace*" (Daniel 2:34,35 NKJV).

Simply stated, if the Roman Empire were fully revived today to the point of its greatest extent, and Jesus returned and fully destroyed it, Babylon, Medo-Persia, and Greece could not be said to be all destroyed 'at the same time.' Although a large portion of the lands held by these empires would be destroyed, roughly two-thirds of all three empires would be left untouched. On the other hand, if the Islamic Caliphate were fully revived today, and Jesus returned and conquered it, then Babylon, Medo-Persia, and Greece could also be said to all be completely destroyed as well. The Islamic Caliphate fulfils the requirements of the text, but the Roman Empire does not. So, the question is: 'Can we now know what was previously unknowable?' Could the unnamed fourth world empire in the Book of Daniel be the Islamic Caliphate?

4

More about Daniel's Fourth World Empire

We've been thinking of how the prophet Daniel was told to seal up the message that he'd been given by God (or at least the last part of it). It was to be a message capable of being truly understood only when the time of its fulfilment was approaching. The question we're asking ourselves is this: has that time now arrived? It has always intrigued me, for one, why Daniel never identified the fourth empire that was to come to rule or dominate the world in the sequence of four great world empires commencing in turn from the year 600 BC and running onwards to the time of the end of world empires. Why does he name in turn the Babylonian, the Medo-Persian and the Greek empires but then simply talk of the 'fourth' empire?

In chapter two, Daniel interprets king Nebuchadnezzar's dream. Its message from God was that in God's program for world history, three empires would succeed Nebuchadnezzar. This was seen from the vision the king received of a giant statue made from four metals of decreasing value when descending

18

from head to toe: gold, silver, bronze and finally legs of iron. Here's the explanation of the vision:

> *"Then there will be a fourth kingdom as strong as iron; just as iron smashes and crushes everything, so, like iron that crushes, it will smash and crush all these things. And in that you saw the feet and toes, partly of potter's clay and partly of iron, it will be a divided kingdom; but it will have within it some of the toughness of iron, since you saw the iron mixed with common clay. And just as the toes of the feet were partly of iron and partly of pottery, so some of the kingdom will be strong, and part of it will be fragile. In that you saw the iron mixed with common clay, they will combine with one another in their descendants; but they will not adhere to one another, just as iron does not combine with pottery"* (Daniel 2:40-43).

We can observe a few features straightaway. The fourth kingdom was to be a divided kingdom of crushing brutality. In its final form or at the end of its existence it would consist of 10 parts in some kind of confederation presumably, but of a mixed nature. Now we should first notice that this is a Babylon-centered program, one that's outlined here to the Babylonian king. The empires following him encompassed the city of Babylon at their very heart. In that sense the influence of the city of Babylon would live on. The seventeenth and eighteenth chapters of the final book of Revelation confirm that at the end of time Babylon will again come to dominate. Now let's return to Daniel's words to the Babylonian king:

> *"You continued watching until a stone was broken off without hands, and it struck the statue on its feet of iron and clay, and crushed them. Then the iron, the clay, the bronze, the silver, and the gold were crushed to pieces **all at the same time**, and they were like chaff from the summer threshing floors; and the wind carried them away so that not a trace of them was found. But the stone that struck the statue became a great mountain and filled the entire earth"* (Daniel 2:34).

A final thing to observe from the text is how all the metals representing all four of the world empires that would come to dominate the world successively were to be crushed to pieces all at the same time. We might well wonder how this could be possible if one empire followed another over thousands of years of earth history. Their final destruction is shown to Daniel to be brought about by the return of Christ who will yet set up his kingdom on this earth and rule over it. When he smashes the last and future expression of the fourth empire, it is said that all are crushed to pieces at the same time. This can only be the case if there is something connecting all four, something common to all, something that survives from one to another. From the starting point of the Babylonian king Nebuchadnezzar as the head of gold to the final demise of the great city Babylon as foretold in Revelation, it would seem likely that the city of Babylon itself is that link. Again, in the seventh chapter of Daniel's prophecy, the same message is given to Daniel himself directly but in the place of the four metals, we have four beasts:

"Then I desired to know the exact meaning of the fourth beast, which was different from all the others, exceedingly dreadful, with its teeth of iron and its claws of bronze, and which devoured, crushed, and trampled down the remainder with its feet, and the meaning of the ten horns that were on its head, and the other horn which came up, and before which three of the horns fell, namely, that horn which had eyes and a mouth uttering great boasts, and which was larger in appearance than its associates. I kept looking, and that horn was waging war with the saints and prevailing against them, until the Ancient of Days came and judgment was passed in favor of the saints of the Highest One, and the time arrived when the saints took possession of the kingdom. "This is what he said: 'The fourth beast will be a fourth kingdom on the earth which will be different from all the other kingdoms, and will devour the whole earth and trample it down and crush it.

As for the ten horns, out of this kingdom ten kings will arise; and another will arise after them, and he will be different from the previous ones and will humble three kings. And he will speak against the Most High and wear down the saints of the Highest One, and he will intend to make alterations in times and in law; and they will be handed over to him for a time, times, and half a time. But the court will convene for judgment, and his dominion will be taken away, annihilated and destroyed forever. Then the sovereignty, the dominion, and the greatness of all

> *the kingdoms under the whole heaven will be given to the*
> *people of the saints of the Highest One; His kingdom will*
> *be an everlasting kingdom, and all the empires will serve*
> *and obey Him.'* *"At this point the revelation ended. As*
> *for me, Daniel, my thoughts were greatly alarming me*
> *and my face became pale, but I kept the matter to myself"*
> (Daniel 7:19–28).

This was another visionary representation of the final form of world empire before Christ's return to earth to rule, and it appalled Daniel. Again, it's depicted not only as bestial but exceedingly dreadful. In the place of ten toes we now have ten horns but the same idea is being presented. Its period of dominion extends right up until the return of Christ, but this is not counted as a fifth empire. The only way to read this is that this is a re-emergence of the same fourth empire. In its final form, this fourth world empire is the evil empire of the Antichrist, soon to become fully apparent, but even now its identity is becoming clear as we approach the time of the end of world empires. The meaning of Daniel's writing is finally being exposed to those who search to and fro among his pages that they might increase in knowledge.

The fourth kingdom has to be Babylon-centric and savagely cruel. We've begun to witness barbaric cruelty in modern times, have we not? The same city that has been a base of operations serving past middle-eastern empires will be found at the end to be still ruling over the kings of the earth (Revelation chs. 17 & 18). A confederation of ten nations (perhaps those listed in Psalm 83) will give their allegiance to one supremely powerful dictator. The Bible imagery of this supreme leader is that of a horn: that was the ancient symbol of power. These nations will be united in their hatred of Israel. Perhaps it's not without significance that the root words of 'Arabian' and 'mixed' look identical (see Daniel 2:41)?

We noted before: the fourth kingdom will be a divided kingdom of crushing brutality. The Muslim world been inherently divided over whom it recognises as being Mohammed's rightful successor. That rift between Shias and Sunnis has never been bridged. Muslims are fighting Muslims today in the Yemen, for example. The conflict there is maintained as a proxy war, in effect, between Iran on the one side and the Saudis on the other. Shias versus Sunnis. Saudi's hostility with Iran has even caused it to make diplomatic gestures towards Israel, their common enemy. When Daniel (in ch.11) was given a later vision of more detailed prophetic history of the third empire, with some still future foreshadowings, he saw Israel squeezed between the 'king of the north' and the 'king of the south.' This may well be the shape of things still to come.

5

Someone Known As 'The Assyrian'

Many of us are familiar with the "Christmas texts" of Isaiah and Micah. By this I mean:

> *"For a Child will be born to us, a Son will be given to us; and the government will rest on His shoulders; and His name will be called Wonderful Counselor, Mighty God, Eternal Father, Prince of Peace. There will be no end to the increase of His government or of peace on the throne of David and over his kingdom, to establish it and to uphold it with justice and righteousness from then on and forevermore. The zeal of the LORD of armies will accomplish this"* (Isaiah 9:6-7).

> *"But as for you, Bethlehem Ephrathah, too little to be among the clans of Judah, from you One will come forth for Me to be ruler in Israel. His times of coming forth are from long ago, from the days of eternity"* (Micah 5:2).

What we often fail to emphasize is the context of these verses. Just 3 verses later in Micah's prophecy we read:

> *"This One will be our peace. when the Assyrian invades our land, when he tramples on our citadels, then we will raise against him seven shepherds and eight leaders of people. They will shepherd the land of Assyria with the sword, the land of Nimrod at its entrances; and He will rescue us from the Assyrian when he invades our land, and when he tramples our territory* (Micah 5:5-6).

The same thing is found back in Isaiah's writings surrounding the much-loved verse we opened with:

> *"Woe to Assyria, the rod of My anger and the staff in whose hands is My indignation, I send it against a godless nation and commission it against the people of My fury to capture spoils and to seize plunder, and to trample them down like mud in the streets. Yet it does not so intend, nor does it plan so in its heart, but rather it is its purpose to destroy and to eliminate many nations"* (Isaiah 10:5-7).

And later, we read:

> *"The LORD of armies has sworn, saying, 'Certainly, just as I have intended, so it has happened, and just as I have planned, so it will stand, to break Assyria in My land, and I will trample him on My mountains. Then his yoke will be removed from them, and his burden removed from their shoulders. This is the plan devised against the entire earth;*

> *and this is the hand that is stretched out against all the*
> *nations. For the LORD of armies has planned, and who*
> *can frustrate it? And as for His stretched-out hand, who*
> *can turn it back?'"* (Isaiah 14:24-27).

While we readily identify the references to our Messiah in Isaiah and Micah, it's far less common to have 'the Assyrian' likewise identified as the Antichrist. Throughout Isaiah's prophecy, we see this same Messiah-versus-Assyrian theme repeated several times. There are a few names by which the world's final dictator is known in the Bible. One of the lesser known ones for the Antichrist is 'the Assyrian.' The theme of the Assyrian is found primarily in the books of Isaiah and Micah. Both of these prophets prophesied in great detail about both Jesus the Messiah and the Antichrist. The theme that runs through the prophecies of both Isaiah and Micah is the final conflict between Jesus the Messiah and the Antichrist, who throughout these prophecies is referred to again and again as 'the Assyrian.'

The fuller context of some of the most famous messianic prophecies in all of Scripture revolves around the theme of the conflict between Jesus and the Antichrist. In Isaiah 13–23, after prophesying the coming judgment against the Antichrist, we're given a list of many of the nations that will be destroyed or judged along with the Antichrist when the Messiah comes to bring the promised victory to his people. The thing of interest is that whichever nation one may point to today within the territory once occupied by the former Assyrian Empire, they are all of the same majority religious persuasion.

Obviously, Isaiah's prophecies had a meaning for the people of God at or near the time of writing. In the 8ᵗʰ and 7ᵗʰ centuries BC, the Assyrian empire was the world superpower, and as such was the major threat to God's people, Israel, at that time. In Second Kings chapter 18, we famously read of God's deliverance of Judah from the Assyrian king Sennacherib after Hezekiah, Judah's king, had prayed to God for his direct intervention. And that's what happened, of course.

Scripture uses a historical king from the ancient Assyrian Empire as a type of foreshadowing of the coming Antichrist. Isaiah's 'Assyrian,' as he spoke of him then, controlled much of what we refer to today as eastern Turkey, as well as parts of Syria and Iraq. In studying these biblical prophecies, we can make a correlation or connection between the ancient names and peoples and their last-days ultimate fulfilment – and the connection we can use is that of keeping the same general geographic location. In other words, we locate the geographical area being referred to in Bible times, and while letting that remain constant, we simply update to the modern names for the same region. That's the best way of applying the golden rule of Bible interpretation that says first ask what the Bible's message meant to its original hearers, and then evaluate what it means to us today. We may expect any contemporary meaning to be consistent with the original meaning.

It's striking that, although Daniel made no mention of the Assyrian, since he was writing later in history, nevertheless he writes of the *"king of the North"* (Daniel 11). This was someone his prophecies looked forward to who would rule over the territory of the old Seleucid Empire, which would also come to include today's Turkey, Syria, and Iraq (also included, as we saw, within the more ancient Assyrian empire's territory). Although the Bible prophets were writing at different times, and describing events in terms of different empires that were either contemporary with them or which they saw prophetically as coming to dominate the centuries lying ahead, their descriptions of current and future events do blend seamlessly together. What is above all fascinating is that although they paint things using different terms, they all point to the same man, from the same region, with the same motivations. They're all references to the Antichrist, a.k.a. the Assyrian or the king of the north. And they all point to the Middle East and North Africa as the chief targets of God's judgment at the time of Jesus' return.

As we see the alignment of power blocks in the Middle East today, and the religious, ideological connection between them, rereading these ancient prophecies should give us much food for thought.

6

The People of the Coming Prince

One of the verses that has been at the centre of biblical prophecy relating to the end of world empires is Daniel chapter 9 and verse 26. We should, as always, read it in its context. The context is God's program for his people, Israel. This program is in 70 units, usually translated as '70 weeks' although that can be somewhat confusing until we as Daniel's readers get used to the idea that each unit of seven is not an actual literal week, that is not a week of seven days, but a so-called 'week' of 7 years. Where this can be seen most clearly is in the final Bible book of Revelation which makes it explicit that half of the final week of the same program amounts to 42 months or, in other words, three and a half years. We may assume that there's consistency throughout God's entire prophetic program for Israel, meaning that seventy of these weeks equals 490 years.

The confirmation of this is found in the fact that Daniel was writing of these things while in exile. That historic exile, the period of Israel being away from their promised land, was plainly stated as lasting for 70 years (see Daniel 9:2; Jeremiah 25:11,12).

God explained that this specific time gap was related to the fact that in Israel's chronic disobedience they'd failed to observe the practice of allowing their land to remain fallow or unused for one year in every seven. And so, God demanded all the 'land sabbaths' that had been missed for the previous 490 years. One year in every seven from the 490 in total, which makes 70. The land would have all the missing rest periods due to it all at once for the whole of Israel's exile away from it. What we're saying is that at the time of Daniel, God in judgement had been looking back over 490 years, and equally now in prophecy he was looking forward over 490 years, these are the 70 'sevens' or 'weeks' of Daniel's prophecy.

> "Seventy weeks have been decreed for your people and your holy city, to finish the wrongdoing, to make an end of sin, to make atonement for guilt, to bring in everlasting righteousness, to seal up vision and prophecy, and to anoint the Most Holy Place. So you are to know and understand that from the issuing of a decree to restore and rebuild Jerusalem, until Messiah the Prince, there will be seven weeks and sixty-two weeks; it will be built again, with streets and moat, even in times of distress. Then after the sixty-two weeks, the Messiah will be cut off and have nothing, and the people of the prince who is to come will destroy the city and the sanctuary. And its end will come with a flood; even to the end there will be war; desolations are determined. And he will confirm a covenant with the many for one week, but in the middle of the week he will put a stop to sacrifice and grain offering; and on the wing of abominations will come the one who makes desolate,

until a complete destruction, one that is decreed, gushes forth on the one who makes desolate" (Daniel 9:24-27).

We notice that there's a further subtlety here. The seventy weeks are split into 7 plus 62 plus one. At the end of the 7 plus 62 weeks, so at the end of 69 weeks, Christ was crucified. After this, and concerning the city where Christ was crucified, we read of *"even to the end there will be war."* We find ourselves still living in that period today. Jerusalem isn't at peace. It's currently divided and troubled. Then we read that *"the prince who is to come"* will make a seven-year peace deal or a covenant for one week. This is clearly someone different from the Messiah who was previously mentioned as having been *"cut off."* This coming prince is yet another way of speaking about the Antichrist. And this final week, Daniel's seventieth, the one that completes God's program for Israel, is the very same seven-year period that's described in great detail between Revelation chapters 6 and 19. In other words, it's future. The end of this seventieth week for Israel will coincide with the time of the end of world empires. This takes place at the time known as the Day of the Lord. Then, at that time, world sovereignty will be restored to Israel, and Christ, the Messiah, will be king over the earth.

What many Bible students have also picked up from this section, and from verse 26 in particular, is a clue as to the identity – or nationality at least – of this future prince known as the Antichrist who will break the deal he earlier brokered with Israel, the deal that will seem to bring peace for a while to the troubled Middle East. What's that clue we're talking about? Well, we're told that in historical times after Christ's death, the people of the coming prince, would destroy Jerusalem and its temple. This means we need to examine the historical data behind the events of AD 70 when this actually happened as had been predicted. Forces then under the command of the Roman General, Titus, ransacked and burned Jerusalem.

Notice it's the people of the prince we're interested in. It could so easily be assumed that most of the soldiers Titus commanded at that time were Italians or Europeans. However, both historical testimony and the consensus of modern scholarship tell us that very few of the soldiers who destroyed the Temple and Jerusalem in AD 70 were actual Europeans. This is significant, as *"the people* [Hebrew: 'am] *of the prince"* doesn't refer to the kingdom or empire under which the people lived, but rather it refers to the people themselves. Before the Roman Empire became an empire, it was called the Roman Republic. In the early days of the Republic, the majority of the soldiers/legionnaires recruited to serve in the Roman armies/legions were Italians from Rome and the nearby regions. As the Empire expanded, it became impossible to man the entire Empire with soldiers only from Italy.

At the beginning of the first century, Emperor Augustus made a series of sweeping reforms that led to dramatic changes in the ethnic make-up of the Roman armies. After Augustus' reforms in AD 15, the only portion of the Roman army that continued to consist largely of Italians from Rome proper was the Praetorian Guard, an elite military unit whose job was to specifically guard the emperor and the tents of the generals. The remainder of the army was increasingly composed of what were known as 'provincials,' citizens who lived in the provinces—the outer fringes of the Empire, away from the capital of Rome. This happened with all the Roman legions of this time period, but most certainly it was the case for the Eastern legions used to attack Jerusalem.

Publius Cornelius Tacitus was both a senator and a historian of the Roman Empire. Speaking of the Roman attack of Jerusalem, Tacitus detailed the specific legions and the peoples that made up the attacking army: "Titus Caesar ... found in Judaea three legions, the 5th, the 10th, and the 15th ... To these he added the 12th from Syria, and some men belonging to the 18th and 3rd, whom he had withdrawn from Alexandria. This force was accompanied ... by a strong contingent of Arabs, who hated the Jews with the usual hatred of neighbors." (The History Bk. 5 chap.1)

Titus Flavius Josephus, another historian from this period, confirms Tacitus's report: "So Vespasian sent his son Titus [who], came by land into Syria, where he gathered together the Roman forces, with a considerable number of auxiliaries from the kings in that neighborhood." (De Bello Judaico, Ed. B. Niese vii libri 3.8; Malchus 3.68 & De Bello Judaico, Ed. B. Niese vii libri 5.40 & See also Wars of the Jews 5.1.6 e-sword app). He later mentioned Malchus, the king of Arabia, as one of those kings who supplied Arab soldiers. Again, he revealed that the Roman legions used to attack Jerusalem were stationed in Syria. All of these legions would have consisted of a majority of Eastern soldiers: Arabs, Syrians, Egyptians, etc.

This means that the soldiers in the Eastern provinces that destroyed Jerusalem and the Temple were in fact Eastern peoples—the inhabitants of Asia Minor, Syria, Arabia, and Egypt. In other words, they were the ancestors of the modern-day inhabitants of the Middle East. Josephus tells us: "The multitude of the Arabians, with the Syrians, cut up [those who deserted Jerusalem], and searched their bellies [for silver or gold coins they'd swallowed]... in one night's time about two thousand of these deserters were thus dissected." (De Bello Judaico, Ed. B. Niese vii libri 5.551). This shows us that *"the people of the prince"* were not Europeans, but Middle-eastern peoples. In this case, the indicated ethnicity of the future world leader can be updated from European to Middle-eastern.

Let's recap - we've seen that one day as Daniel was reading the book of the prophet Jeremiah (Daniel 9:2), he saw something he'd not understood before. God had decreed that their current captivity would last 70 years – 70 years of enforced rest on the land of Israel because for the past 490 years his people had failed to observe its 'land sabbaths' (2 Chronicles 36:21). But then, looking forward, the 490 years that now stretched ahead in God's program for Israel were divided up – in the same way – as 70 groups of 'sevens'. Here then is the vision God gave to Daniel (9:24-27): *"Seventy weeks have been decreed for your people and your holy city, to finish the transgression, to make an end of sin, to make atonement for iniquity, to bring in everlasting righteousness, to seal up vision and prophecy, and to anoint the most holy place."*

This obviously hasn't happened yet as far as Israel is concerned. So the entire 490 years weren't consecutive from that time. The first question is: 'When did they begin?' Verse 25 answers that: *"So you are to know and discern that from the issuing of a decree to restore and rebuild Jerusalem until Messiah the Prince there will be seven weeks and sixty-two weeks ...*" This decree to restore Jerusalem was the one which was later given in 444 BC by Artaxerxes in the 20th year of his reign (Nehemiah 2:1,5): "*Then **after** ... the Messiah will be cut off.*" The Messiah being 'cut off' refers to the crucifixion of Jesus Christ. While it was to take place 'after' the completion of the 69 weeks, the wording avoided saying that it was 'during' the 70th week (indicating a gap between the 69th and 70th weeks. When the best historical dates are used for Artaxerxes' decree and for the death of Jesus, it can indeed be shown that there are precisely '69 weeks' between them.) But when the Jews crucified Jesus, the Messiah whom God had sent, it was as though Daniel's clock stopped ticking. In other words, the final seven years of the prophecy, the '70th week', hasn't happened yet. The events of the Book of Revelation are future – but soon to begin.

7

A Multi-force Invasion of Israel

Not all Arabs are Muslims. It's also worth remembering that a Middle Eastern country like Iran has a mainly Persian – not Arabic – population. We mustn't forget those differences between the labels Middle Eastern, Arabic and Muslim. As far as the Middle East is concerned, what about the great swathe of Islamic countries from the central Asian republic of Kazakhstan right round to the Western Sahara of northern Africa? To the south and west, as well as to the east and north of Israel, there's an impressive, wide arc of predominantly Islamic countries.

Do Bible prophecies have anything to say about this? From Israel's point of view, it must seem like an intimidating swathe of countries that sweeps down from Kazakhstan through Iran, Iraq, Saudi Arabia and on to Algeria and her Saharan neighbours. Just how real is any threat to Israel? Does the Bible indicate hostility against Israel coming from this quarter? The key section is found in Ezekiel's prophecy:

"And the word of the LORD came to me saying, Son of man, set your face toward Gog of the land of Magog, the prince of Rosh, Meshech, and Tubal, and prophesy against him, and say, 'Thus says the Lord GOD, "Behold, I am against you, O Gog, prince of Rosh, Meshech, and Tubal. And I will turn you about ..."

These names probably don't mean much – if anything – to us. The key question is which parts of the world did they refer to at the time when the prophecy was written? These place names were attached back then to the areas we know of today as Turkey, and the countries between the Black and Caspian Seas like Armenia, Azerbaijan, Georgia, and the southern tip of Russia along with north-western Iran. It's a fascinating focus on Turkey. Turkey looks west and east in today's world. It is recognized as a key player in the region. Its government has in the recent past maintained close ties with the west, but on account of its Islamic population it has also begun to look eastwards for support. It was active (1989) in promoting the Black Sea Economic Cooperation Zone, a 'common market' with Armenia, Azerbaijan, Georgia and Russia alongside Turkey. In addition, Turkey has obvious cultural and religious ties with Central Asian countries (former Soviet Republics) like Kazakhstan and Turkmenistan. What is interesting is that today we can see some kind of alliance emerging between countries which the Bible predicts will ultimately be in alliance with each other.

More than that, they will be the leaders of an invasion against

Israel, as prophesied by Ezekiel. For he spoke of an attack on Israel carried out by people who would be living in the general area of Turkey and the land between the Black and Caspian Seas. But Ezekiel (38:5-8) goes on to mention other nations who will join with those countries:

> *"Persia, Ethiopia, and Put with them, all of them with shield and helmet; Gomer with all its troops; Beth-togarmah from the remote parts of the north with all its troops – many peoples with you. Be prepared, and prepare yourself, you and all your companies that are assembled about you, and be a guard for them."*

Heading this second list is Persia which is modern-day Iran. Iranians today speak the Persian (or Farsi) language. Next in line to be mentioned by Ezekiel is 'Cush.' Earlier in his prophecy (29:10), Ezekiel has shown that by Cush he's referring to an area south of Egypt in the region known to us as Sudan and Ethiopia. Then there is 'Put' which is generally accepted as being Libya, to the west of Egypt. Students of Bible prophecy have been scratching their heads for a long time over this unlikely assortment of countries seemingly indicated by Ezekiel long ago. What would Turkey and some former republics of the Soviet Union have in common with Iran, Sudan and Libya? Why should they conspire together to launch an attack on Israel? The best answer now emerging may seem to be Islam, and the rise of Islamic fundamentalism.

A report surfaced in an Arab language magazine some time back which claimed that Iran used the confusion following the collapse of the Soviet Union to purchase nuclear weapons from Kazakhstan. Iranian influence is also growing in Sudan. Apparently, it sent its Revolutionary Guards to train the Sudanese army as well as to supply military equipment. And, of course, Libya's opposition to Israel is well known. Turkey, Iran, the Muslim republics, Sudan and Libya. Countries with little in common – except their Islamic faith – and the fact that Ezekiel implicates them in an attack on Israel. For thousands of years this alliance seemed improbable, but it seems as if at last a grouping – with Turkey and Iran as prime movers – may indeed be starting to show signs of coming together. The big question, of course, is when will any attack take place? Coming back to Ezekiel's prophecy again, we find:

> *"After many days you will be summoned; in the latter years you will come into the land that is restored from the sword, {whose inhabitants} have been gathered from many nations to the mountains of Israel which had been a continual waste; but its people were brought out from the nations, and they are living securely, all of them"* (Ezekiel 38:1-8 NASB).

It is something of a puzzle to know quite when this prediction of Ezekiel applies. It is said to be at a time when Israel feels secure. *'The land ... restored from the sword ... [will be] living securely.'* Weighing all of Ezekiel's clues (37:24-26; 38:8,23; 39:9, 21-23), it may be better to set this among the Lord's judgements of the nations **after** the time when he himself has come as a deliverer to Zion. It is then that LORD *"makes himself known in the sight of many nations."* A time when Israel may be described as *"the land* *restored from the sword."* Besides that, we have already seen a pattern to Ezekiel's writing – one which seems to set out a series of events in relative time sequence. These prophecies about this coalition of forces coming against Israel are sandwiched between Ezekiel's vision of Israel's revival – pictured in the valley of dry bones (ch.37) – and his vision of what we take to be the future Millennial Temple (ch.40).

In the chapter before we read of this attack, we're told that God's Spirit will take up Israel and they will be fully gathered into their land and united as one undivided nation (Ezekiel 37:14,21,22). God will be in their midst and the nations will know it (Ezekiel 37:23,27,28). Do these things not require the return of Jesus Christ to this earth to bring them about? And come he will – to reign for a thousand years. The apostle John in his vision of the future in Revelation 20:1-15 saw an angel who:

> *"... laid hold of ... Satan, and bound him for a thousand years... And I [John] saw thrones, and they sat upon them, and judgment was given to them. And I saw the souls of those who had been beheaded because of the testimony of Jesus and because of the word of God, and those who had not worshiped the beast or his image, and had not received the mark upon their forehead and upon their hand; and they came to life and reigned with Christ for a thousand years. The rest of the dead did not come to life until the thousand years were completed. This is the first resurrection ... when the thousand years are completed, Satan will be released from his prison, and will come out to deceive the nations which are in the four corners of the*

earth, Gog and Magog, to gather them together for the war; the number of them is like the sand of the seashore. And they came up on the broad plain of the earth and surrounded the camp of the saints and the beloved city, and fire came down from heaven and devoured them. And the devil who deceived them was thrown into the lake of fire ..." (NASB)

Firstly, let's again notice the fact that there will be those who will be saved during the great tribulation, having refused to receive the Antichrist's mark and worship his image. They are part of this first resurrection (relative to the Millennium). Also, from the Lord's parable of the separation of the sheep from the goats (Matthew 25:32–34), we note that as well as those who have been raised and judged worthy of entrance into Christ's Millennial kingdom, there will be those who are alive on earth when the Lord returns to the earth – people in ordinary bodies – who will be admitted into the kingdom too. From among the ranks of this latter category (and their descendants) will come this final revolt by Gog and Magog. We underline this to clarify that once any are raised in their new bodies and enter into blessedness, there is no prospect of them ever again succumbing to sin.

It's really interesting that at the close of this one thousand years of peace nations again described as 'Gog and Magog' are said to gather to besiege Jerusalem. If this was the same attack that Ezekiel described, it would hardly seem that the current trends we noted earlier could have any bearing on it. But if the thousand years of peace end with an attack from this region, is it not even more probable that it begins with one as well? This is what we are suggesting, for the Millennium follows on from the most turbulent of times when God's judgements on the nations are still being carried out. In which case, the modern alliances between countries with a common Islamic heritage could well be a factor. However, if the timing of the attack is in doubt, the outcome is not in any doubt. For Ezekiel says of Israel's attackers: *"You shall fall on the mountains of Israel, you and all your troops, and the peoples who are with you; I shall give you as food to every kind of predatory bird and beast of the field"* (Ezekiel 39:4 NASB).

8

The Unmasking of the Antichrist

Bible-believing Christians know that history is headed some-where. One day Jesus Christ will judge the nations at the beginning of his thousand-year reign on this earth. The same person whom the first century Jewish leaders judged to be an impostor, and had crucified on a cross, will return to this earth in glory and rule the nations with a rod of iron (Revelation 12:5). As the Bible prophet, Isaiah, predicted: a king shall reign in righteousness (Isaiah 32:1) and the earth will enjoy peace and all of nature will be in harmony:

> *"The cow and the bear shall graze; their young ones shall lie down together; and the lion shall eat straw like the ox. The nursing child shall play by the cobra's hole, and the weaned child shall put his hand in the viper's den. They shall not hurt nor destroy in all My holy mountain, for the earth shall be full of the knowledge of the LORD as the waters cover the sea"* (Isaiah 11:7-9).

We should acknowledge that not all Christians follow the same approach to the interpretation of Bible prophecy. The difference is most marked when it comes to dealing with the symbolism of the Book of Revelation (the Apocalyptic genre). Some simply see it as an epic poem extolling the final victory of good over evil. In more detail, there have been four different views regarding the book of Revelation. The 'idealist' view, already referred to, teaches that Revelation describes in symbolic language the battle throughout the ages between God and Satan and good against evil. The so-called 'preterist' view teaches that the events recorded in the book of Revelation were largely fulfilled early on – by AD 70 with the fall of the Jerusalem Temple. The unusual word 'preterist' comes from an old term signifying what is past. The 'historicist' view teaches that the book of Revelation is a symbolic presentation of Christian history beginning in the first century AD and continuing through to the end of the age. The prophecies of Revelation are seen by those who favour this view as being fulfilled in various historic events such as the fall of the Roman Empire, the Protestant Reformation, and even the French Revolution.

The 'futurist' view, as its name suggests, teaches that the book of Revelation prophesies events that' will take place in the future, and is the viewpoint we are following. Futurist beliefs usually have a close association with terms like Premillennialism that describe future events occurring in a particular order, with the so-called 'Rapture' of the church, followed by seven years of tribulation for those left behind on earth, and then a thousand-year reign of Christ upon the earth. This is based on a literal approach to interpretation of the Bible and is the approach which maintains a distinction between Israel and the Church and God's respective purposes for each. We can know, on the authority of God's Word, the Bible, that:

1. Christ will return to the air for His Church; and that
2. The Antichrist will afterward rise to power; and so
3. Earth will have unprecedented trouble; and then
4. Christ will return to the earth itself; and
5. He will rule for one thousand years; then
6. Christ will judge unbelievers; when finally
7. A new world will be created.

Confidence for a lot of that general sequence can be drawn out from Paul's writing in 2 Thessalonians 2:

"Now we ask you, brothers and sisters, regarding the coming of our Lord Jesus Christ and our gathering together to Him, that you not be quickly shaken from your composure or be disturbed either by a spirit, or a message, or a letter as if from us, to the effect that the day of the Lord has come. No one is to deceive you in any way! For it will not come unless the apostasy comes first, and the man of lawlessness is revealed, the son of destruction, who opposes and exalts himself above every so-called god or object of worship, so that he takes his seat in the temple of God, displaying himself as being God.

Do you not remember that while I was still with you, I was telling you these things? And you know what restrains him now, so that he will be revealed in his time. For the mystery of lawlessness is already at work; only He

> *who now restrains will do so until He is removed. Then that lawless one will be revealed, whom the Lord will eliminate with the breath of His mouth and bring to an end by the appearance of His coming; that is, the one whose coming is in accord with the activity of Satan, with all power and false signs and wonders, and with all the deception of wickedness for those who perish, because they did not accept the love of the truth so as to be saved* (2 Thessalonians 2:1-10).

Consistent with the list of events that we shared earlier, Paul here begins by talking first about the return of the Lord for his Church when he starts by saying: *"the coming of our Lord Jesus and our gathering together to Him."* This is before he introduces the term *"the Day of the Lord."* Any of his readers familiar with the Old Testament would recognise this wording, for it appears some two dozen times in the writings of the Old Testament prophets. There, it's usually associated with God's final judgements on his people and the nations of the world, often in respect of how they've treated Israel. This Day of the Lord, having begun with judgement, extends to include the time when the Lord will rule over this earth in righteousness and justice. Paul is here confirming to the Thessalonians that certain things must precede this time. Understanding this in the orderly way Paul sets it out here, certainly leads us to the Premillennial view. Between his mention of the Rapture of Christians and the onset of the Day of the Lord, Paul says we're to expect both the Apostasy and the Antichrist.

There's always been speculation about who the Antichrist may be. People play around with the numerical value attributed to people's names, but it's all vain speculation, for we're told the *mystery* of lawlessness must precede the *man* of lawlessness. This is the Antichrist. There's a definite hint here that his identity will not be disclosed until the time is ripe for him to assume the reins of power. Paul then says something that's most intriguing in verses 6 and 7: *"And you know what restrains him now, so that he will be revealed in his time. For the mystery of lawlessness is already at work; only He who now restrains will do so until He is removed. Then that lawless one will be revealed."* We might wish Paul hadn't been quite so cryptic! But God in his wisdom clearly doesn't want us to know all the details. He's not looking to satisfy our sense of curiosity, but rather to simply assure us that all things must move in line with his script, even when to us it may appear as if the world is spiralling out of control. If the Thessalonians knew the nature and identity of this restraining influence, that would appear to be more than we do. Paul does say that while he'd been with them he was telling them about these things. Those other conversations are not recorded in the Bible. We can safely conclude then that we don't need to know the details.

However, there's one thing that catches the eye, certainly if we should happen to check with a more literal translation of Paul's Greek. And that is this: those words *"He who now restrains will do so until He is removed"* may more literally be rendered as 'Until out of its midst he emerges or becomes.' That leads me to think of the restrainer as not being the Church or even the Holy Spirit, but as more likely being some system of governance under Satan's control. Some sense of accountability appears then to be broken, possibly when the man of lawlessness breaks the future peace covenant that will come to be made with Israel. This will have brought a peace respite to the volatile politics of the Middle East for a short time. But Israel, being surrounded on north, east and south by people who for ethnic and religious reasons have no love for her, was never going to be in a stable situation for long under those conditions. A breaking point will come. The restraint of the covenant agreement will be broken. One leader will then emerge in his true colours. He displays himself as God. That likely means he will then turn against the apostate religious system on which he rode to power (see Revelation 17:16). Conceivably then, the dominant Middle Eastern ideology may be betrayed from within by someone who previously had been its high profile figurehead. All this takes place before the Day of the Lord. It's then the Lord Jesus will return to this earth in flaming fire and judgement, as mentioned in the chapter immediately before this.

9

The End of World Empires

Some time back, a US political commentator by the name of Fukuyama spoke of 'the end of history' in relation to the end of 'the Cold War'; the overthrow of tyrants and the prospect of a new world order built from a coalition of nations. The phrase was memorable, but its optimism was unfounded. A golden age of peace dividends hasn't materialized. We've not reached the end of all history, but we may be getting close to the end of world empires. The pieces of the Bible's prophetic puzzle are clicking into place. What the Bible has long foretold as being the shape of things to come is now beginning to materialise.

There's quite a remarkable feature of the Apostle Paul's first letter to the Thessalonians - every chapter ends by focusing on our Lord's return. The apostle's application of prophecy was designed to quicken their spiritual pulse, and set their sights beyond the here and now. There's a real sense in which the more we live for the world to come, the better we'll live in this present world. Those early Christians at Thessalonica, and elsewhere, had an advantage over us in that they were much closer than we are to the language in which the New Testament was originally written. In that original Greek language three different words spell out what's going to happen at the Lord's return. And these words are: presence ('parousia'), revelation ('apokalupsis') and manifestation ('epiphaneia'). The first of these words emphasizes not so much the simple fact of the Lord's return but especially his presence with all the Christian believers of this age – although, obviously, he must return first for this actual presence to become a reality. This is the description of this return for believers which the Bible gives us in 1 Thessalonians chapter 4:15-17:

> *"... we who are alive and remain until the coming* [from 'parousia' – the start of the period] *of the Lord will by no means precede those who are asleep. For the Lord Himself will descend from heaven with a shout, with the voice of an archangel, and with the trumpet of God. And the dead in Christ will rise first. Then we who are alive and remain shall be caught up together with them in the clouds to meet the Lord in the air. And thus we shall always be with the Lord."*

The original Greek word *parousia* is often simply translated, as here, as 'coming', but it more fully signifies 'presence' as opposed to 'absence' (precisely as in the everyday sense of Philippians 2:12 when Paul talks about his periods of presence with or alternatively absence from that local church). Our future experience of Jesus' presence – this being 'with the Lord' – begins at the time we have been reading about, which many people refer to as 'the Rapture': which means the 'snatching up of Christ's Church' by Christ himself (our word 'rapture' coming via the Latin rather than directly from the Greek). This 'snatching up' or 'catching up' is in fact a good way to describe what will happen because all believers at the Lord's coming will be caught up in the clouds to meet the Lord in the air. He doesn't at that time come all the way down to the earth. He comes to the air and calls all believers on himself to him. It's then that we, the believers, enter into this specific period of being in his presence.

The Bible talks about things which will take place during his presence with his saints – which is the best way of translating the end of 1 Thessalonians 3:13 (with the emphasis here being on the duration of the period). This special time of his presence with us after the Rapture event will, of course, be hidden from the eyes of the world. Life on this planet will go on after all true Christians have been taken away from it. The salt of the earth will have gone, and the earth will become more and more corrupt. At least seven years will run their course on earth, for the Bible describes them in detail. Terrible judgements and world-wide catastrophes will rock the globe, and the world, or a great many in it, will find themselves looking to a world leader for deliverance; a leader who is quite definitely in opposition to God and his Christ. When his true colours are revealed, it will cost many their lives in trying to escape from him. During all this time, as the earth ripens for God's judgement, the hidden presence of Christ with believers from the Church Age will continue. But then, at a particular moment signalled in advance by God, his presence with us is going to be revealed to the world. It will be dramatically signalled and unveiled before a watching world: *"For as the lightning comes from the east and flashes to the west, so also will the coming* [parousia – here the close of the period is being referred to] *of the Son of Man be"* (Matthew 24:27).

As we've said, *"the coming of the Son of Man"* referred to there is the hidden state of his presence with us which is then ending. For the second key Bible word is the word 'revelation', as we'll see in a moment. A time will come when, after having come for us, the Lord will 'unveil' to the rest of the world his presence with us. As a result of this revelation the glory of the Lord is going to be manifested: it's going to become visible. Those are the three Bible words mentioned earlier: presence, revelation and manifestation. As they apply in our Bibles to the Lord's return, we have first of all this special time of his presence with us in the period after the Rapture when he catches us up to be with himself, hidden from the world. Then comes the moment of revelation to the world as described in Revelation 1:6,7: *"He is coming with clouds, and every eye will see Him, even they who pierced Him. And all the tribes of the earth will mourn because of Him."*

There's no mention of any other than the Lord and the believer in connection with his presence with the Church after he comes and takes it to be with himself. Removed and hidden from the world, we will enjoy his presence with us until the moment when the covering veil is drawn aside (the revealing of Romans 8:19; 2 Thessalonians 1:7) and the Lord Jesus is revealed to the world in flaming fire from heaven. The effect of this revelation will be that the presence of Christ which we've been enjoying will become visible – or manifest – to the whole world, for the Bible talks of *"the brightness of His coming"* (2 Thessalonians 2:8). It's at that time the words of Colossians 3:4 find their fulfilment: "*When Christ who is our life appears* [or is made manifest], *then you also will appear with Him in glory.*" To see it in the orderly two-stage way the Bible presents it, we need to distinguish between those words: presence, revelation and manifestation. The manifestation of the glory of the Lord is the result of the revelation, and what is being revealed or unveiled is his presence which will have been with us ever since the event known as 'the Rapture of the Church.'

I hope these thoughts about this first prophetic event for which we, as believers, are waiting, will fill us with a sense of assurance; for they were designed to do just that for the first century believers at Thessalonica and elsewhere. As well as inspiring our worship, a consideration of Bible prophecy is clearly meant to stimulate such a sense of hope and encouragement in us. And there are more good biblical reasons to look into the prophetic sections of the Bible. For example, the apostle Peter was even more explicit in saying how knowledge of the future is meant to shape our lives now. When he spoke of the world to come, he stressed it was so that his readers might know what sort of people they ought to be in holy conduct and godliness (2 Peter 3:11).

There are other reasons to believe that our Lord's Second Coming will take place in two phases with the tribulation period (see Matthew 24:21) sandwiched between the Rapture of Christians and Christ's return to the earth to reign. These include the four biblical 'I will' covenants in the Old Testament, and these are:

- The Abrahamic (Genesis 12 ff.)
- The Palestinian (Deuteronomy 30)
- The Davidic (2 Samuel 7), and
- The New Covenant (Jeremiah 31)

All of these – if taken literally – mean that God still has unfinished business with Israel (confirmed by the big picture of Romans 11). In turn, this means the Church has not replaced, nor will ever replace, Israel in God's plans. For one thing, the Lord is not currently on the throne of David – which is something Luke 1:32 says is to be expected. The Lord is currently at the right-hand of the Father on heaven's throne, but that's not the throne of King David. This present age is no golden age on earth, so we are still 'pre-Millennial.' Those who don't take a pre-Millennial view rely on a spiritualizing method of interpretation to:

1. deny the strict distinctions between Israel and the church, and also
2. deny the doctrine of imminence, all because they
3. deny the literal approach to Scripture.

So far, as we think of the birth, life, death and resurrection of our Lord Jesus, he has fulfilled all the relevant prophecies in an exact and literal manner. There is absolutely no reason to expect this to change for the remainder.

About the Publisher

Hayes Press (www.hayespress.org) is a registered charity in the United Kingdom, whose primary mission is to disseminate the Word of God, mainly through literature. It is one of the largest distributors of gospel tracts and leaflets in the United Kingdom, with over 100 titles and many thousands dispatched annually. In addition to paperbacks and eBooks, Hayes Press also publishes Golden Bells, a popular daily Bible reading calendar in wall or desk formats.

If you would like to contact Hayes Press, there are a number of ways you can do so:

By mail: c/o The Barn, Flaxlands, Royal Wootton Bassett, Wiltshire, UK SN4 8DY

By phone: 07341 379815

By eMail: info@hayespress.org

via Facebook: www.facebook.com/hayespress.org

About the Author

Born and educated in Scotland, Brian worked as a government scientist until God called him into full-time Christian ministry on behalf of the Churches of God (www.churchesofgod.info). His voice has been heard on Search For Truth radio broadcasts for over 40 years (visit www.searchfortruth.podbean.com) during which time he has been an itinerant Bible teacher throughout the UK. His evangelical and missionary work outside the UK is primarily in Belgium, The Philippines and South East Central Africa. He is married to Rosemary, with a son and daughter.

Also by Brian Johnston

Here are just a few of the over 100 titles published in the Search for Truth series.

Songs of Zion

This is a valuable little book for anyone who is interested in the worship of God according to the scriptural pattern. Brian traces how Old Testament Israel worshipped their God - the God of Zion - including via the 'songs of Zion' in drawing near to worship at the house of God, and as pilgrims drew near on their upward journey to Jerusalem ('earthly Zion') in the 'Songs of Ascents.' Brian explains from John 4, 1 Peter 2, and Hebrews 3, 10 and 12 how this drawing near to God's physical house has a wonderful counterpart in the New Testament - a spiritual house in which it is possible for obedient believers to draw near in faith to God week by week to worship Him in spirit and in truth in the heavenly Zion.

Can You Profess Christ and Still Be Lost?
The eternal security of our salvation is a hotly debated topic amongst Christians today, Bible teacher and broadcaster Brian Johnston examines what the Bible has to say about whether it is possible to 'fall away' and how God wants us to be sure that we are saved.

- Law and Grace: Two Different Freedoms
- Is It Possible To Be a Carnal Christian?
- Is It a Case of 'No Holiness No Heaven'?
- Are Good Works Required for Salvation?
- Is It Possible to Fall Away?
- It's Not About How To Be Saved
- Is It Possible to Believe the Gospel in Vain?
- Once Saved, Always Saved
- The Different Tenses of Our Salvation

Finding Christ in the Old Testament
"They said to one another, 'Were our hearts not burning within us when He was speaking to us on the road, while He was explaining the Scriptures to us?'" (*Lk.24:27:32*) Burning hearts! The inevitable result of having the Bible explained so it all begins to make sense and the person and work of Christ, its central character, comes into sharper focus.

www.ingramcontent.com/pod-product-compliance
Lightning Source LLC
Chambersburg PA
CBHW061407140726
47997CB00003B/1404